BILL PIBURN PLAYS
ANTONIO CARLOS JOBIM

Recorded by Mark Thornton at Sidekick Sound Studios, Madison, Tennessee
For more information on Bill Piburn and Fingerstyle 360 visit: www.fingerstyle360.com

PLAYBACK+
Speed • Pitch • Balance • Loop

To access audio visit:
www.halleonard.com/mylibrary

Enter Code
3549-5675-3562-0554

ISBN 978-1-4584-2227-9

Visit Hal Leonard Online at
www.halleonard.com

Contact us:
Hal Leonard
7777 West Bluemound Road
Milwaukee, WI 53213
Email: info@halleonard.com

In Europe, contact:
Hal Leonard Europe Limited
42 Wigmore Street
Marylebone, London, W1U 2RN
Email: info@halleonardeurope.com

In Australia, contact:
Hal Leonard Australia Pty. Ltd.
4 Lentara Court
Cheltenham, Victoria, 3192 Australia
Email: info@halleonard.com.au

Brazilian songwriter and vocalist **ANTONIO CARLOS JOBIM** (1927–1994) was one of the creators of the popular song style known as bossa nova. He has been widely acclaimed as one of Brazil's greatest and most innovative musicians of the twentieth century. Often known by the nickname Tom, he was born in Rio de Janeiro on January 25, 1927. He grew up in the seaside southern Rio suburb of Ipanema, later the setting for his most famous song. Jobim was fourteen when he began piano lessons with Hans Joachim Koellrutter, a local music scholar of German background who favored the latest experimental trends in European classical music. Jobim would later point to the influence by French Impressionist composers Claude Debussy and Maurice Ravel on his own music, but a new set of influences was on its way to Brazil in the form of American jazz. Visits to Rio by the Duke Ellington Orchestra and other American jazz bands helped shape Jobim's own compositions.

Antonio Carlos Jobim has reached legendary status and in his native Brazil he is iconic. After all, how many songwriters have an international airport named after them? Jobim passed away on December 8th, 1994 in New York's Mount Sinai Hospital where he was being treated for cardiac disease. His body was returned to Brazil where a four-hour funeral parade was held in Rio de Janerio. In 1991, Antonio Carlos Jobim was inducted into the Songwriters Hall of Fame.

BILL PIBURN

Bill Piburn grew up in a musical family in Kansas City, Missouri. His grandfather, Grant Leonard Piburn, was a violinist who began his career playing in silent movie theaters. His father, James Russell Piburn, was a guitarist and singer who performed from the mid-1950s through the late 1970s. Bill's father gave him his first guitar on his tenth birthday and began to teach him. By the age of fourteen, he was playing in local nightclubs with his father's band much to the dismay of his mother. Bill began classical guitar study at the age of sixteen with Douglas Niedt and by nineteen was selected as one of ten guitarists to study with Christopher Parkening at Montana State University. After a year in Montana, he returned to Kansas City to perform and study jazz with pianist John Elliott. Bill's time with John opened new avenues to understanding harmony and arranging for solo guitar.

Bill has authored seven books and was the editor of Fingerstyle Guitar magazine from 2000 through 2010. He currently publishes his own magazine Fingerstyle 360. His playing has won him praise from guitarists such as Chet Atkins, Earl Klugh, Johnny Smith and Martin Taylor.

DEDICATION:

I dedicate this work to my brother James Arthur Piburn. I am very proud of you!

THANKS:

Thanks to Mark Thornton at Sidekick Sound Studios for the long hours and encouragement.

Special thanks to Jeff Schroedl at Hal Leonard for giving me this project; it was a challenge, yet rewarding. Another few pieces of the puzzle we call the guitar revealed.

TESTIMONIALS:

"I am here listening to the arrangements of Jobim's music by Bill Piburn. I can't wait to pick up my guitar and try to play them! The arrangements are put together with such taste and creativity that Antonio Carlos Jobim himself would be proud. All the elements of a tasteful solo guitar arrangement can be found - good choice of notes, chords, rhythm, counterpoint and played with a nice groove! Bill, I'm a big fan and will definitely be stealing your ideas, my friend. God bless you, the music of Jobim and all the guitar players!

- Sandro Albert, NYC Nov. 26, 2013

"Bill's arrangements are always so musical and thoughtful. They're true works of art, and obviously coming from someone who loves the instrument and understands its voice."

- Kerry Marx – Studio guitarist, Nashville, TN November 10, 2013

"Bill Piburn has created a delightful collection of Jobim's best loved classics, masterfully arranged and performed for solo guitar. Players of all levels and styles will benefit from working through and learning Piburn's technically challenging, yet thoroughly musical arrangements. The best part is we can use them on gigs!"

- Sean McGowan, Assistant Professor and Guitar Program Director, University of Colorado Denver

"I'm very happy and honored to write a quote for Bill's new book on the music of Antonio Carlos Jobim. I grew up in Brazil with Jobim's music so it's very exciting to see a musician like Bill devote himself to creating such meticulous arrangements. They show extremely good taste and interesting ideas that will surely be a reference point for all guitarists who love Jobim's music in a broader vision. In other words, not only Brazilian music known for its exotic rhythms, but as a complete work that now enjoys diverse musical influences that our great maestro Tom Jobim received and synthesized in a unique way. Bill works the arrangements with counterpoint, harmony and melodies that show how our magnificent guitar still has much to be explored and how it can be the protagonist of a reinterpretation of Jobim's work. The arrangements offer those who take advantage intelligently of their content a rich repertoire of ideas and musical information. Congratulations Bill and thanks for the magnificent work!"

- Roberto Taufic, Rome, Italy, Nov. 26, 2013

"Bill Piburn is one of the most experienced and sophisticated arrangers for solo guitar I know. His knowledge of harmony, voice leading, and style is immense, and his ability to apply these things guitaristically in his arrangements is truly impressive."

- Dr. Stanley Yates, Chair of the guitar department, Austin Peay State University, Clarksville, Tennessee

Água de Beber
(Water to Drink)

English Words by Norman Gimbel
Portuguese Words by Vinicius De Moraes
Music by Antonio Carlos Jobim

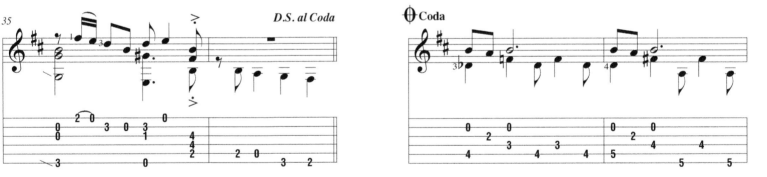

D.S. al Coda

Coda

Chega de Saudade
(No More Blues)

Original Text by Vinicius de Moraes,
Music by Antonio Carlos Jobim

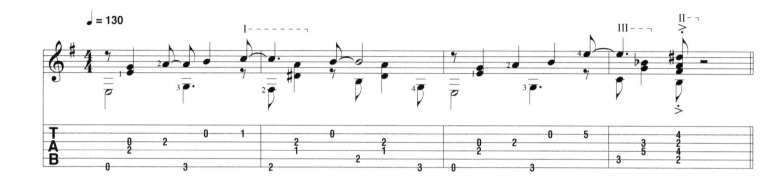

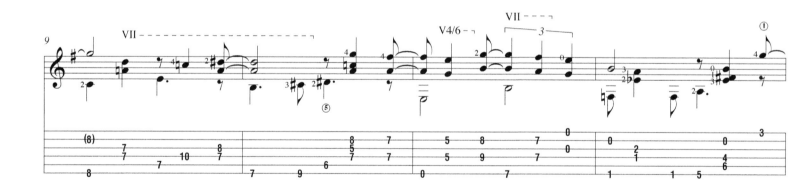

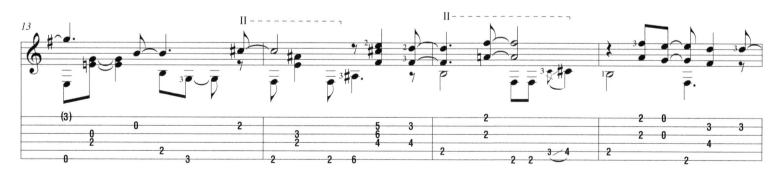

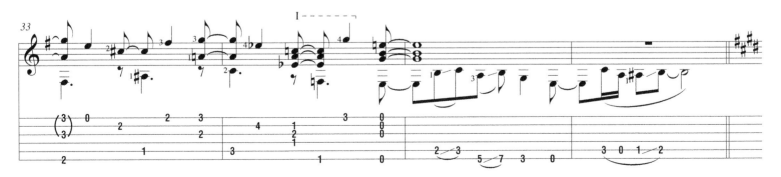

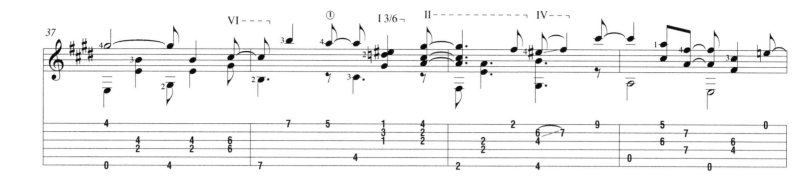

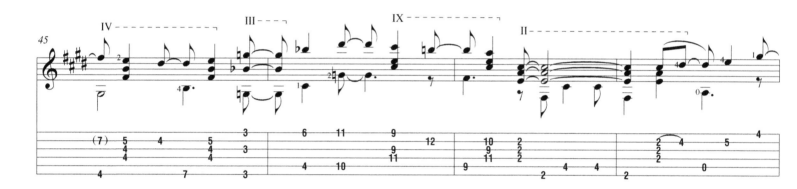

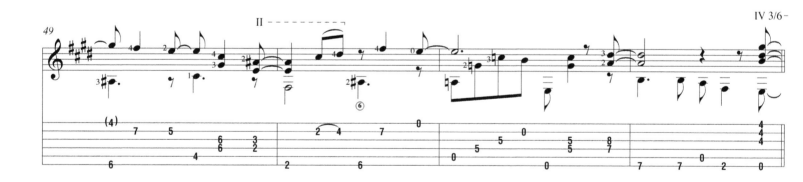

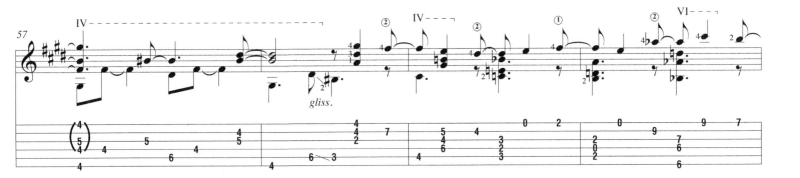

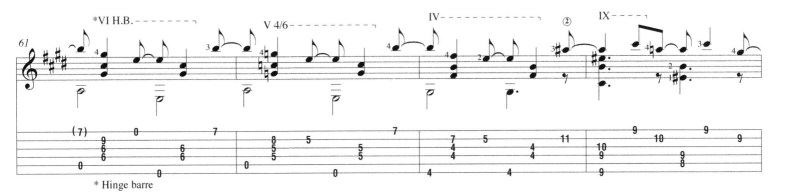

* Hinge barre

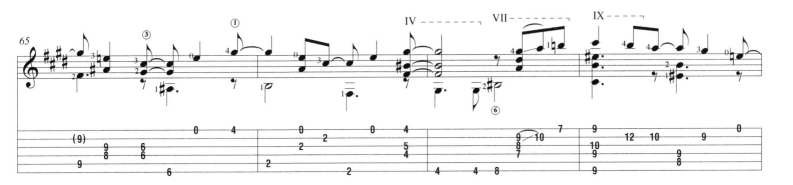

Desafinado

Original Text by Newton Mendonça
Music by Antonio Carlos Jobim

♩ = 117

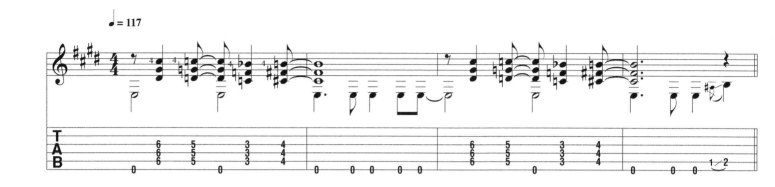

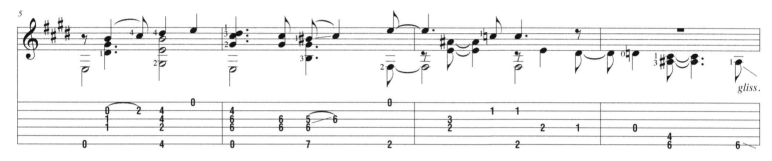

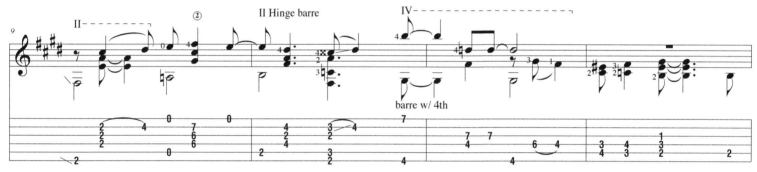

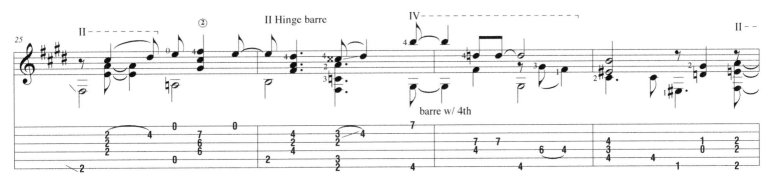

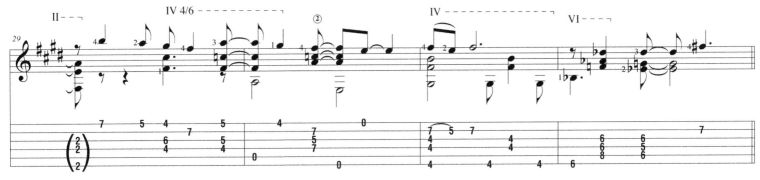

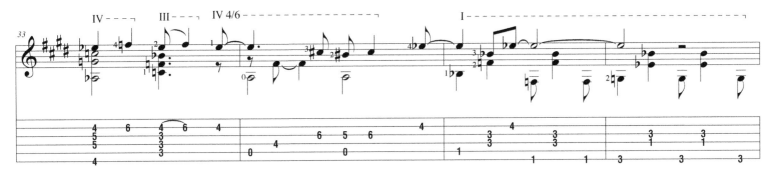

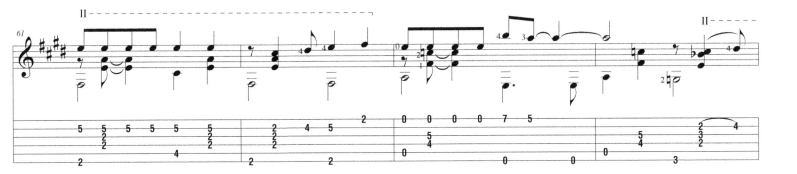

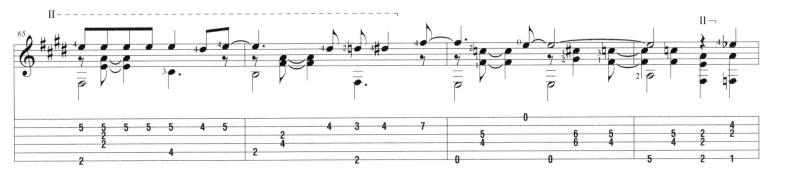

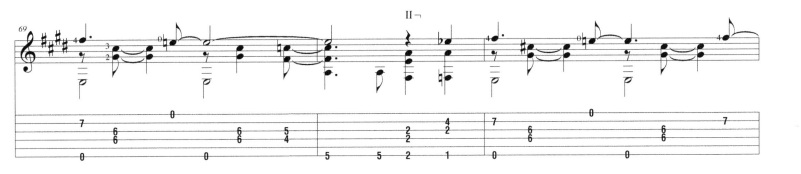

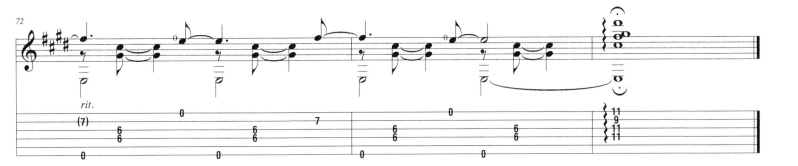

The Girl from Ipanema
(Garôta de Ipanema)

Music by Antonio Carlos Jobim
English Words by Norman Gimbel
Original Words by Vinicius de Moraes

* Harp Harmonic: The note is fretted normally and a harmonic is produced by gently resting the right hand's index finger 12 frets (one octave) above the indicated fret while the right hand's thumb assists by plucking the appropriate string. This technique also applies to unfretted harmonics played at the 12th fret.

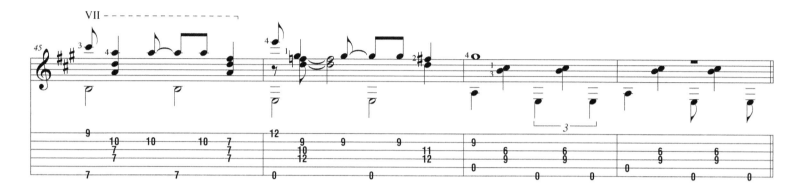

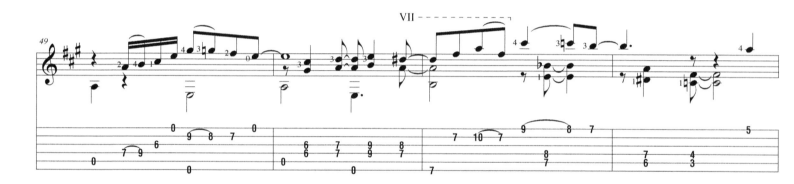

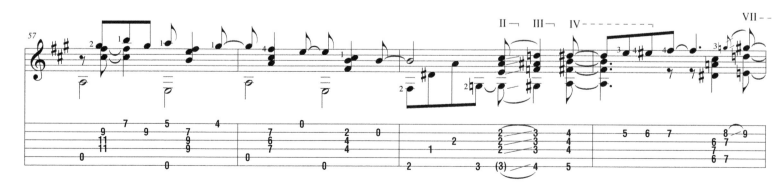

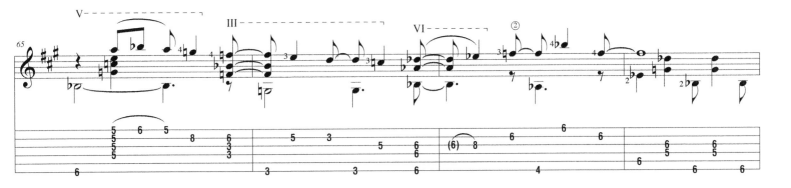

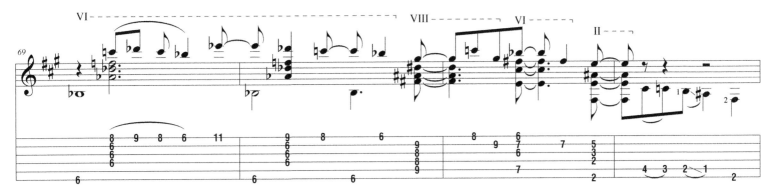

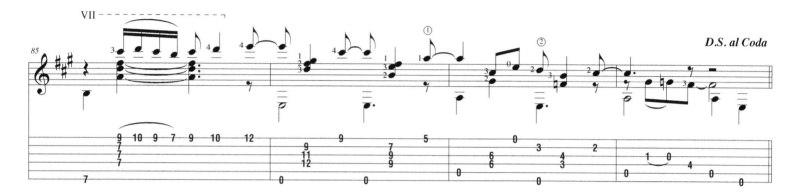

D.S. al Coda

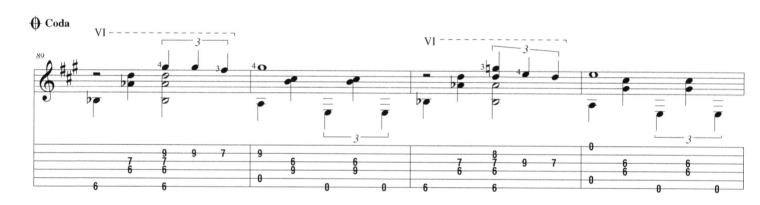

Once I Loved
(Amor em Paz) (Love in Peace)

Music by Antonio Carlos Jobim,
Portuguese Lyrics by Vinicius de Moraes,
English Lyrics by Ray Gilbert

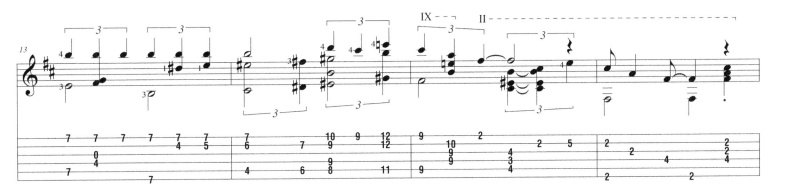

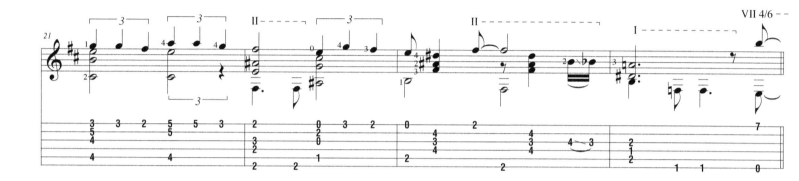

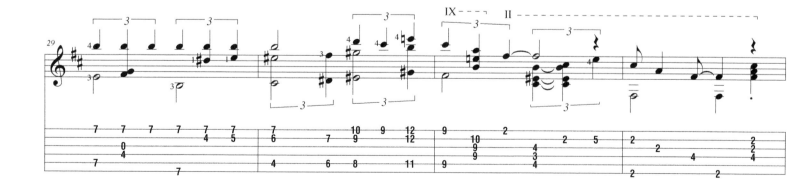

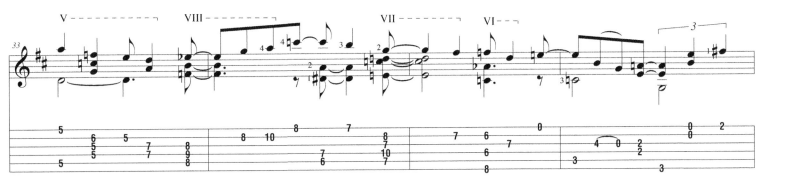

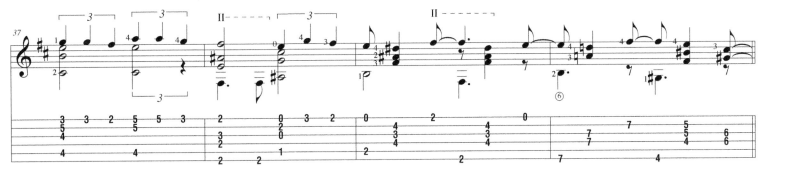

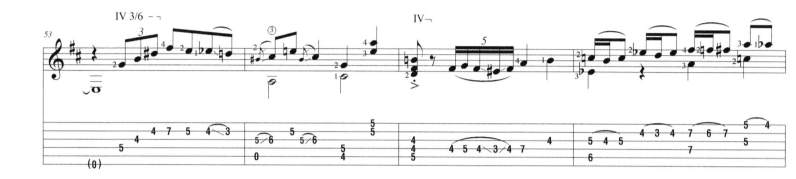

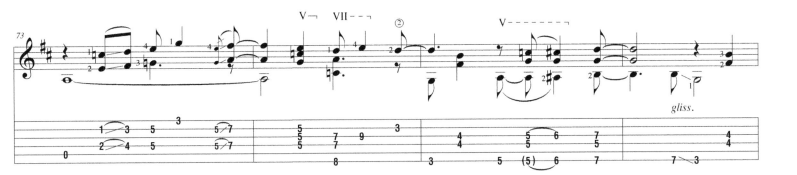

How Insensitive
(Insensatez)

Music by Antonio Carlos Jobim
Original Words by Vinicius de Moraes
English Words by Norman Gimbel

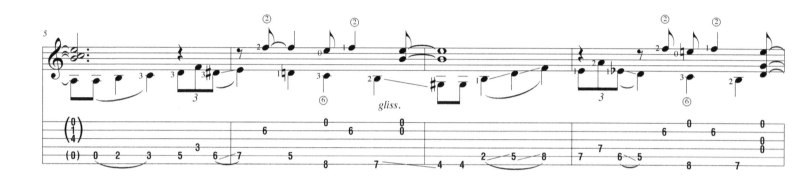

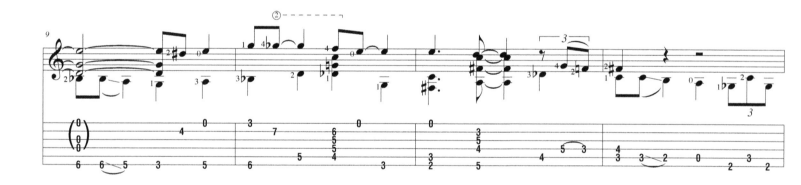

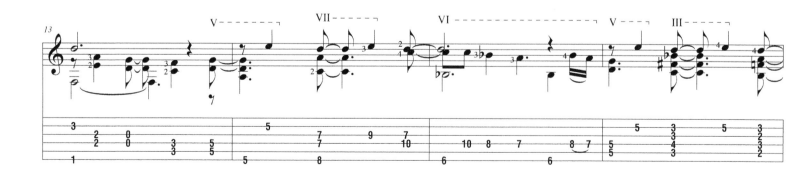

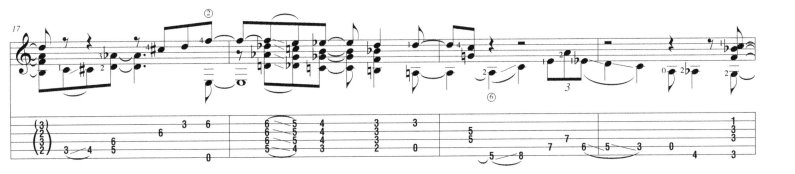

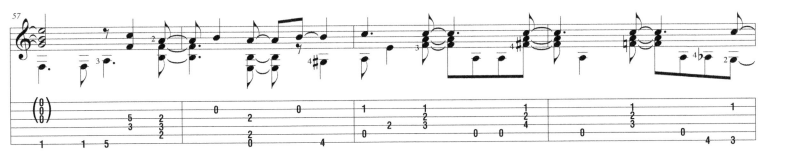

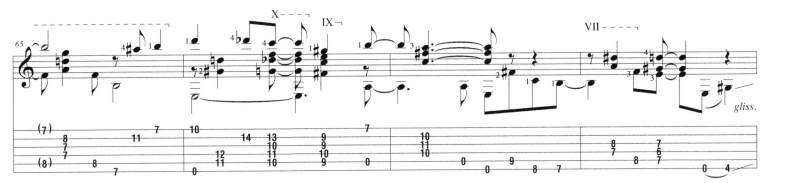

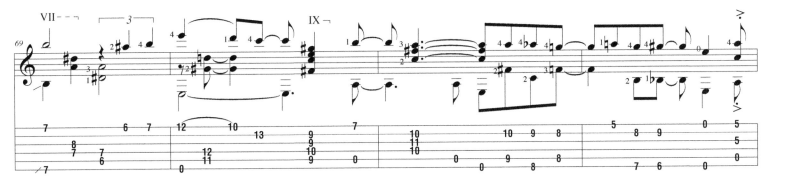

Meditation
(Meditação)

Music by Antonio Carlos Jobim
Original Words by Newton Mendonça
English Words by Norman Gimbel

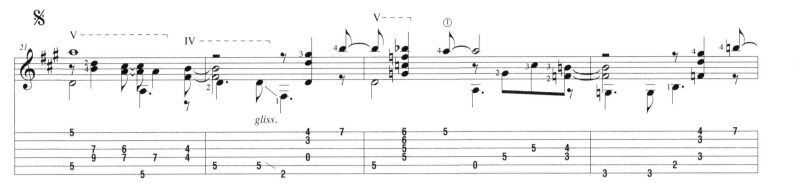

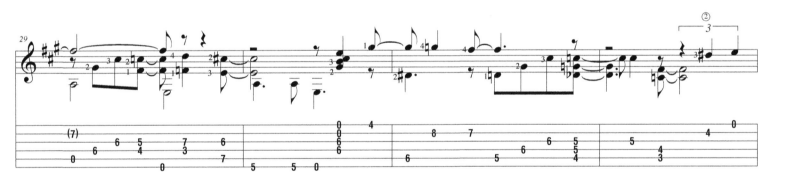

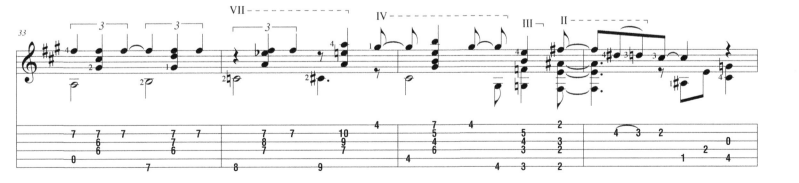

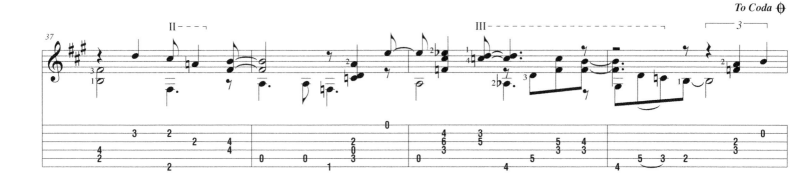

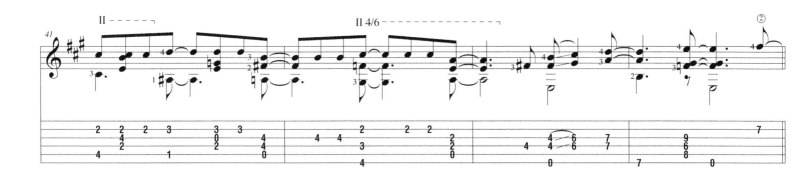

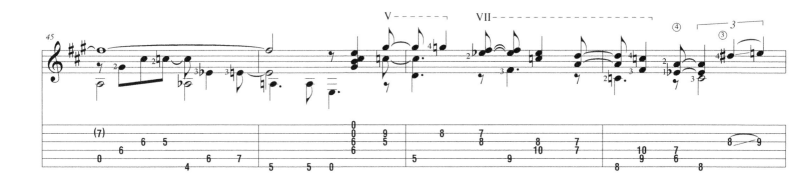

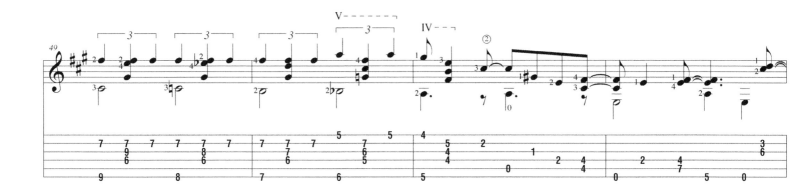

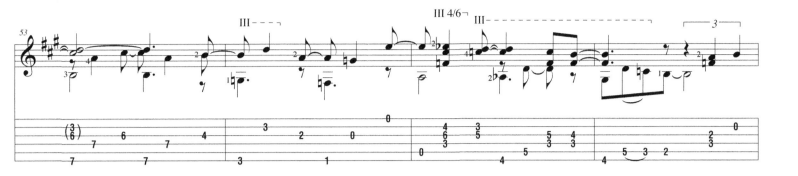

Quiet Nights of Quiet Stars
(Corcovado)

English Words by Gene Lees
Original Words and Music by Antonio Carlos Jobim

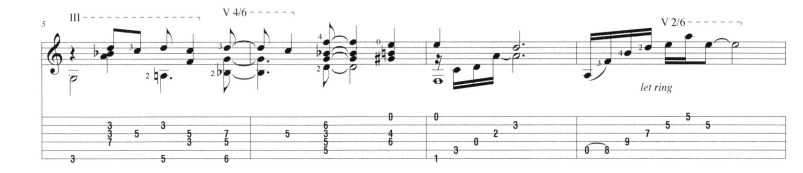

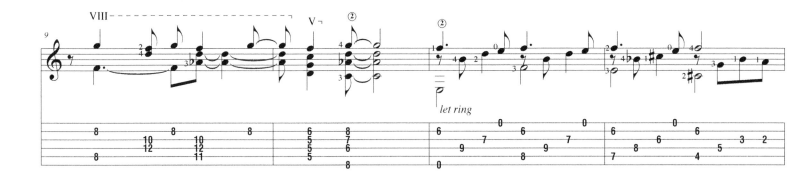

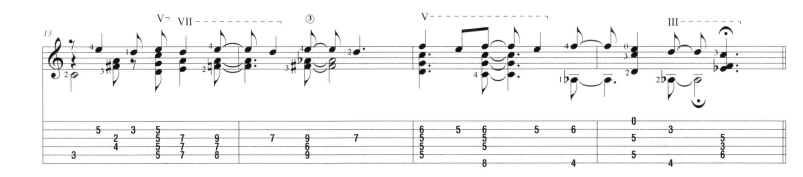

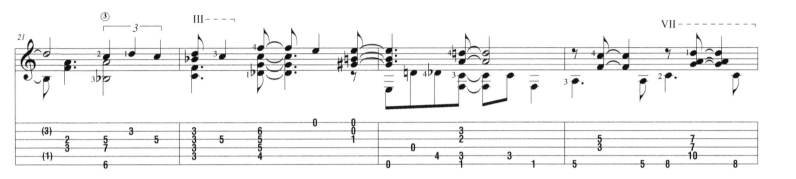

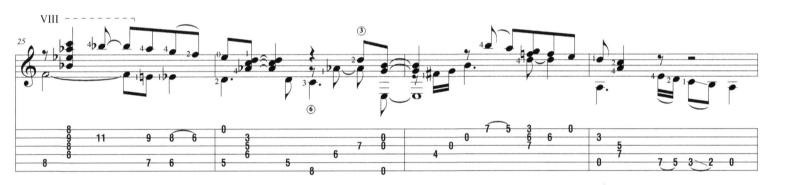

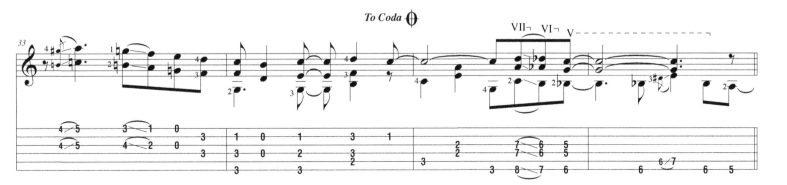

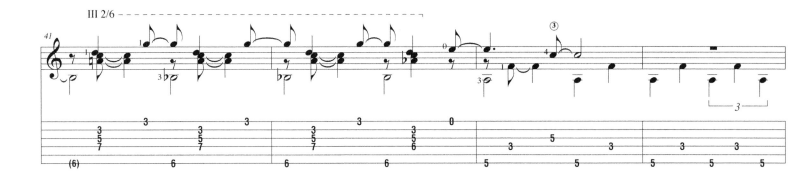

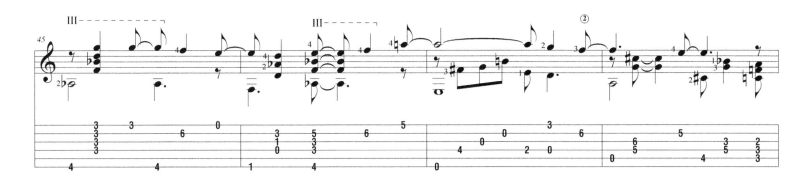

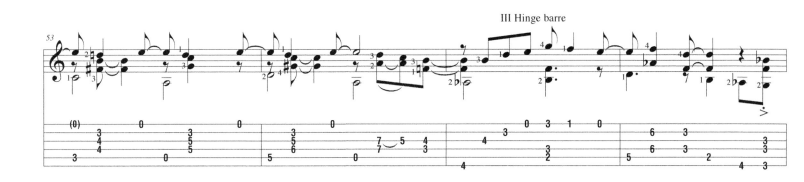

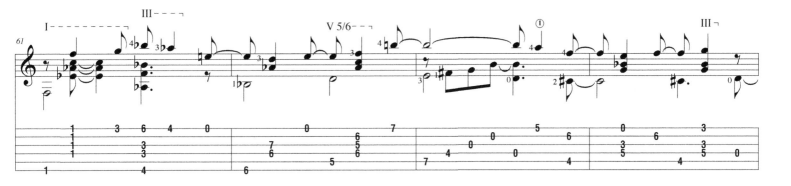

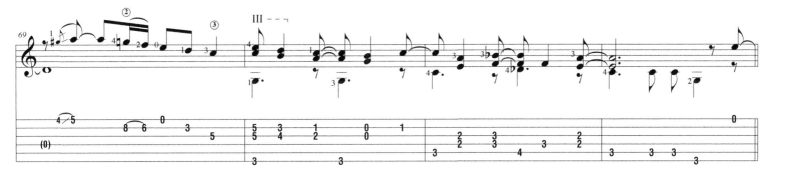

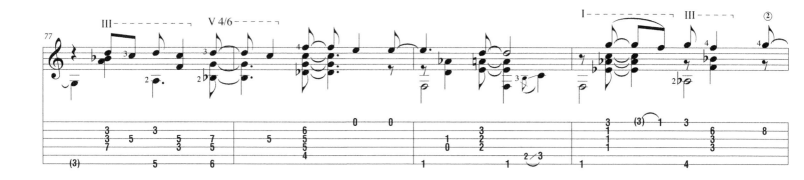

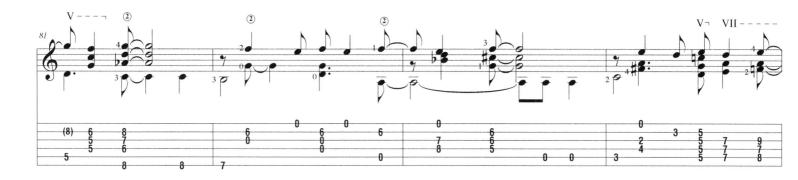

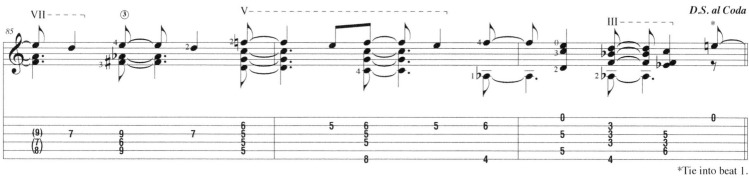

*Tie into beat 1.

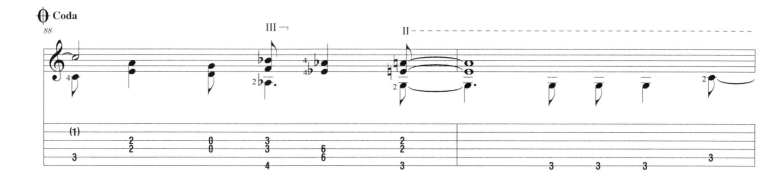

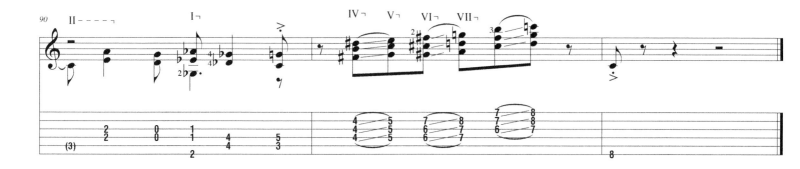

Song of the Jet
(Samba do Avião)

Words and Music by Antonio Carlos Jobim

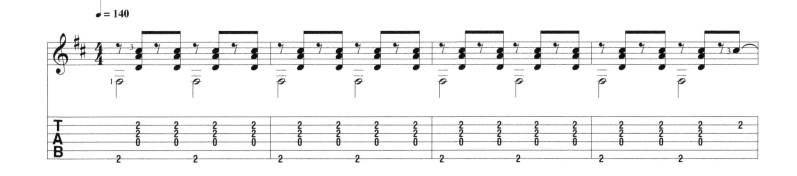

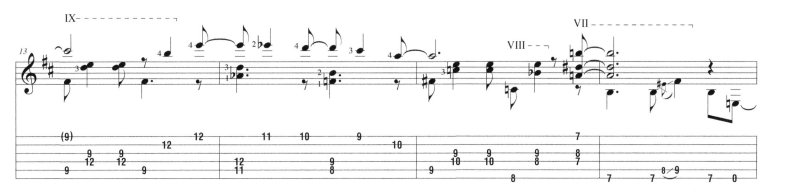

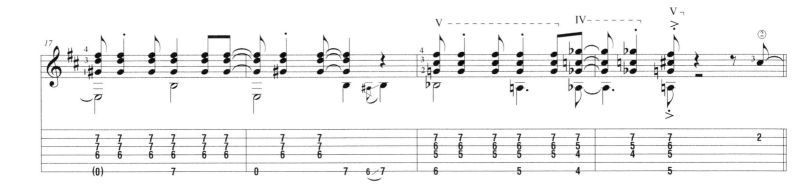

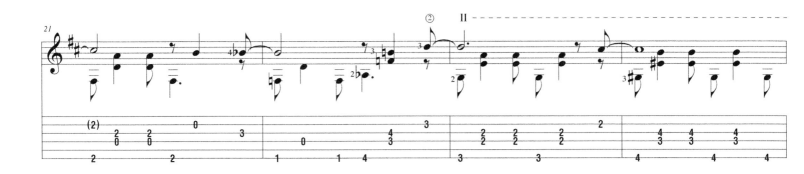

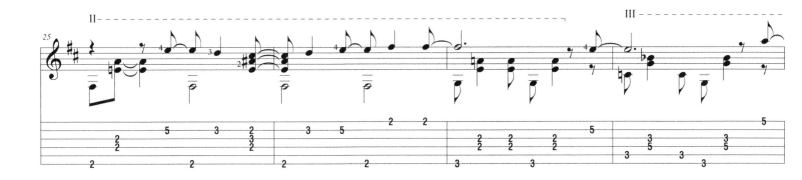

38

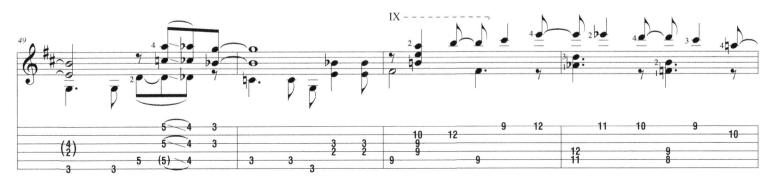

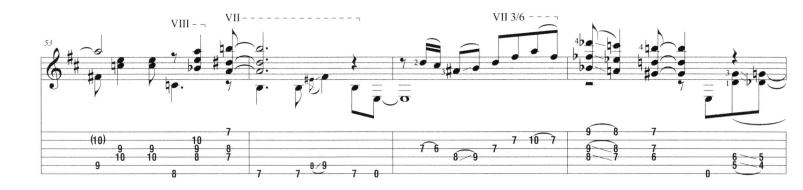

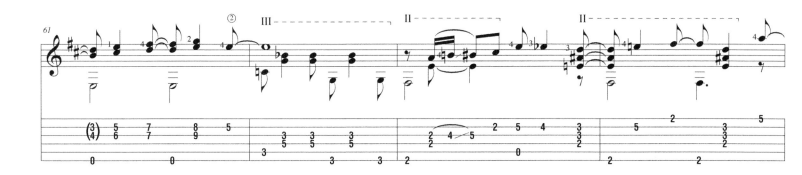

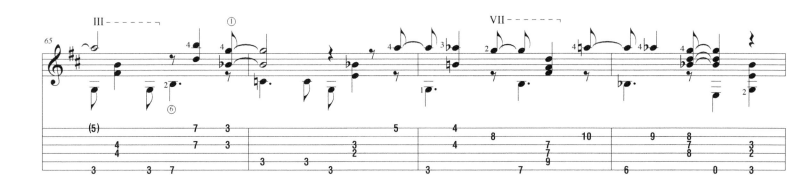

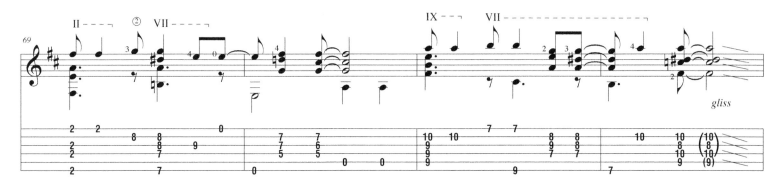

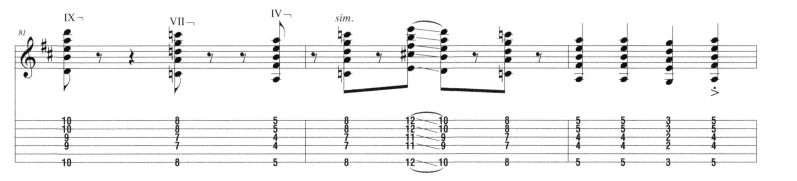

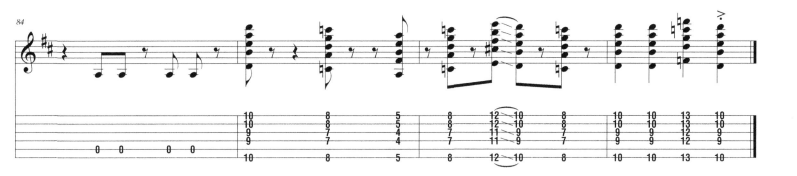

Wave

Words and Music by Antonio Carlos Jobim

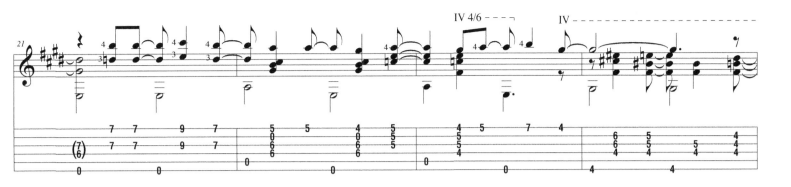

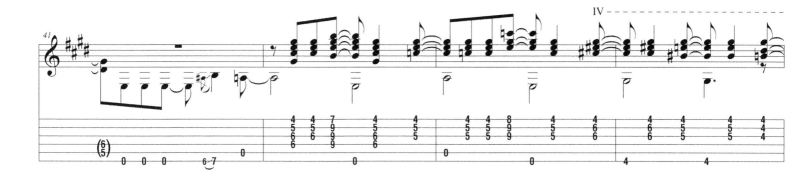

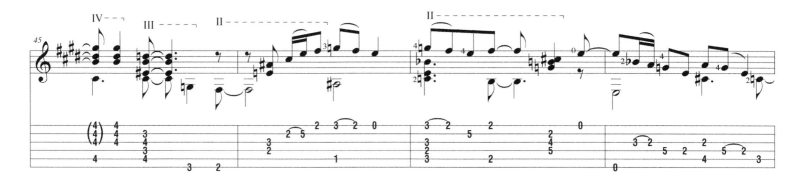

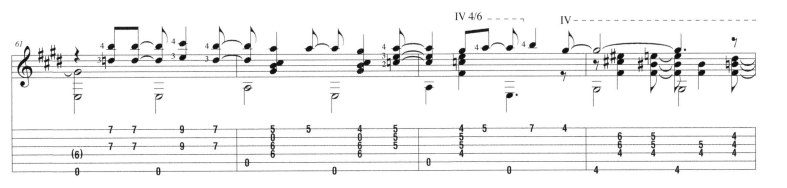

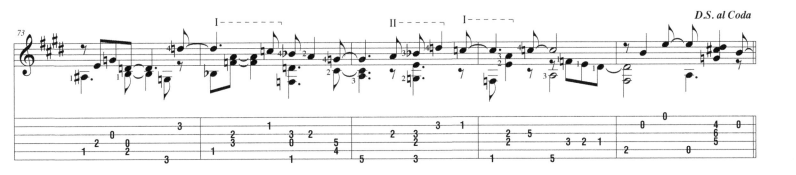

Zingaro

By Antonio Carlos Jobim

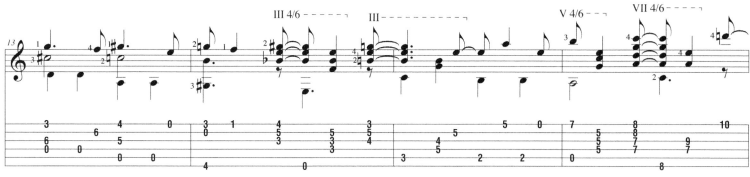

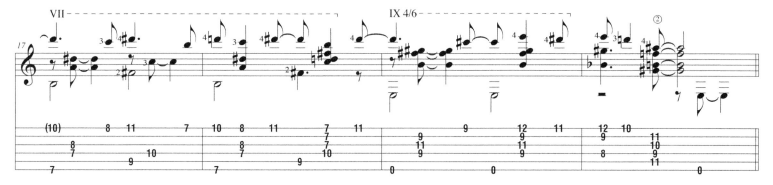

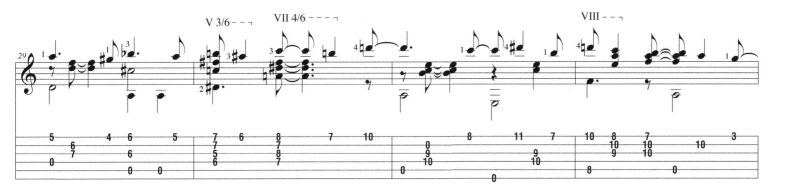

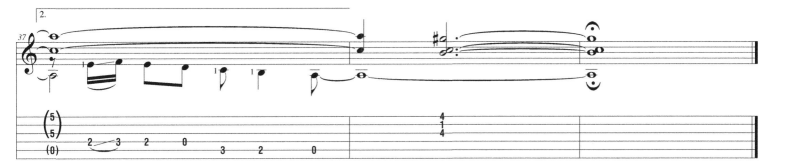

Triste

By Antonio Carlos Jobim

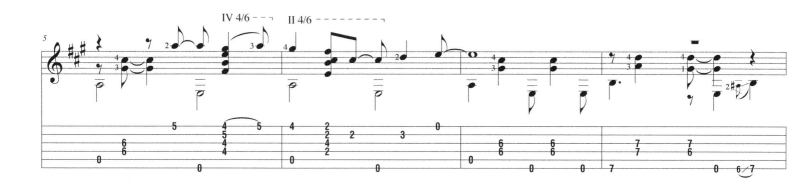

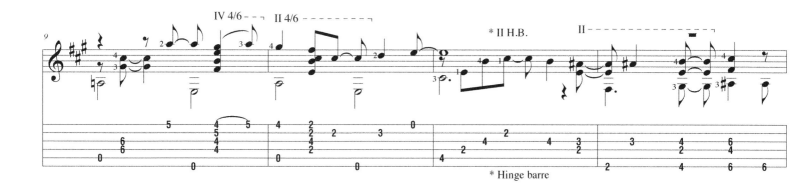

* Hinge barre

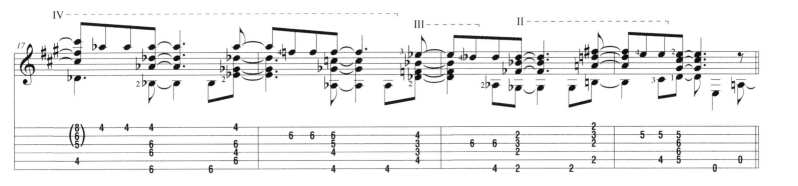

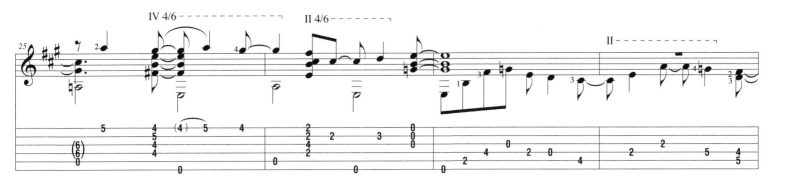

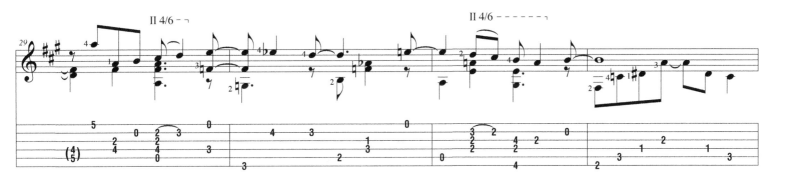

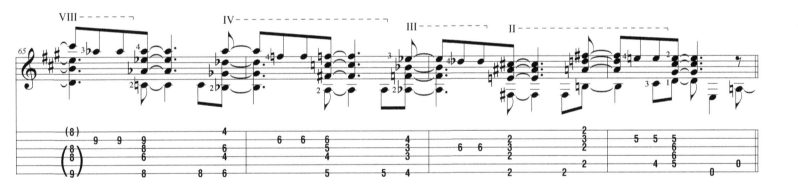

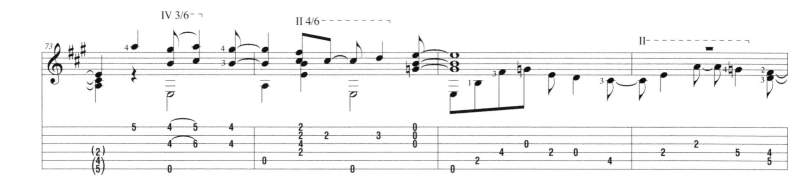

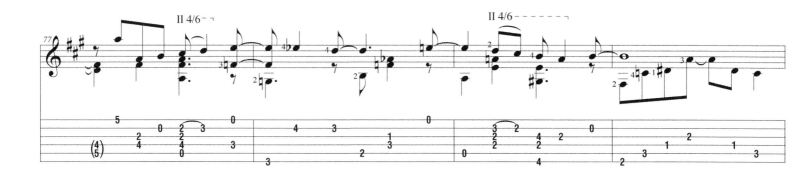

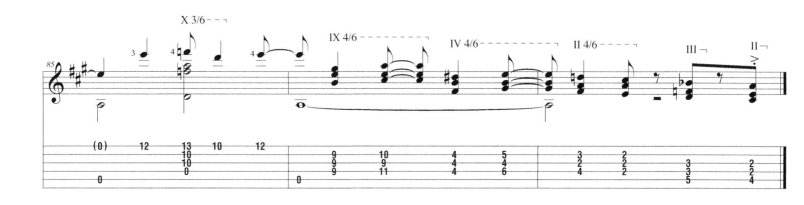

FINGERPICKING GUITAR BOOKS

Hone your fingerpicking skills with these great songbooks featuring solo guitar arrangements in standard notation and tablature. The arrangements in these books are carefully written for intermediate-level guitarists. Each song combines melody and harmony in one superb guitar fingerpicking arrangement. Each book also includes an introduction to basic fingerstyle guitar.

  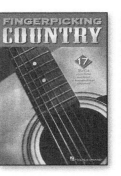 

Fingerpicking Acoustic
00699614 15 songs.......................$14.99

Fingerpicking Acoustic Classics
00160211 15 songs.......................$16.99

Fingerpicking Acoustic Hits
00160202 15 songs.......................$15.99

Fingerpicking Acoustic Rock
00699764 14 songs.......................$16.99

Fingerpicking Ballads
00699717 15 songs.......................$15.99

Fingerpicking Beatles
00699049 30 songs.......................$24.99

Fingerpicking Beethoven
00702390 15 pieces.......................$10.99

Fingerpicking Blues
00701277 15 songs $12.99

Fingerpicking Broadway Favorites
00699843 15 songs.......................$9.99

Fingerpicking Broadway Hits
00699838 15 songs.......................$7.99

Fingerpicking Campfire
00275964 15 songs.......................$14.99

Fingerpicking Celtic Folk
00701148 15 songs.......................$12.99

Fingerpicking Children's Songs
00699712 15 songs.......................$9.99

Fingerpicking Christian
00701076 15 songs.......................$12.99

Fingerpicking Christmas
00699599 20 carols.......................$12.99

Fingerpicking Christmas Classics
00701695 15 songs.......................$7.99

Fingerpicking Christmas Songs
00171333 15 songs.......................$10.99

Fingerpicking Classical
00699620 15 pieces.......................$10.99

Fingerpicking Country
00699687 17 songs.......................$12.99

Fingerpicking Disney
00699711 15 songs.......................$17.99

Fingerpicking Early Jazz Standards
00276565 15 songs $14.99

Fingerpicking Duke Ellington
00699845 15 songs.......................$9.99

Fingerpicking Enya
00701161 15 songs.......................$16.99

Fingerpicking Film Score Music
00160143 15 songs.......................$15.99

Fingerpicking Gospel
00701059 15 songs.......................$9.99

Fingerpicking Hit Songs
00160195 15 songs.......................$12.99

Fingerpicking Hymns
00699688 15 hymns $12.99

Fingerpicking Irish Songs
00701965 15 songs.......................$10.99

Fingerpicking Italian Songs
00159778 15 songs.......................$12.99

Fingerpicking Jazz Favorites
00699844 15 songs.......................$14.99

Fingerpicking Jazz Standards
00699840 15 songs.......................$12.99

Fingerpicking Elton John
00237495 15 songs.......................$15.99

Fingerpicking Latin Favorites
00699842 15 songs.......................$12.99

Fingerpicking Latin Standards
00699837 15 songs.......................$17.99

Fingerpicking Love Songs
00699841 15 songs.......................$14.99

Fingerpicking Love Standards
00699836 15 songs $9.99

Fingerpicking Lullabyes
00701276 16 songs.......................$9.99

Fingerpicking Movie Music
00699919 15 songs.......................$14.99

Fingerpicking Mozart
00699794 15 pieces.......................$10.99

Fingerpicking Pop
00699615 15 songs.......................$14.99

Fingerpicking Popular Hits
00139079 14 songs.......................$12.99

Fingerpicking Praise
00699714 15 songs.......................$14.99

Fingerpicking Rock
00699716 15 songs.......................$14.99

Fingerpicking Standards
00699613 17 songs.......................$15.99

Fingerpicking Worship
00700554 15 songs.......................$15.99

Fingerpicking Neil Young – Greatest Hits
00700134 16 songs.......................$17.99

Fingerpicking Yuletide
00699654 16 songs.......................$12.99

HAL•LEONARD®

Order these and more great publications from your favorite music retailer at
halleonard.com

Prices, contents and availability subject to change without notice.

0123
279

JAZZ GUITAR CHORD MELODY SOLOS

This series features chord melody arrangements in standard notation and tablature of songs for intermediate guitarists.

ALL-TIME STANDARDS

27 songs, including: All of Me • Bewitched • Come Fly with Me • A Fine Romance • Georgia on My Mind • How High the Moon • I'll Never Smile Again • I've Got You Under My Skin • It's De-Lovely • It's Only a Paper Moon • My Romance • Satin Doll • The Surrey with the Fringe on Top • Yesterdays • and more.
00699757 Solo Guitar...........................$16.99

IRVING BERLIN

27 songs, including: Alexander's Ragtime Band • Always • Blue Skies • Cheek to Cheek • Easter Parade • Happy Holiday • Heat Wave • How Deep Is the Ocean • Puttin' On the Ritz • Remember • They Say It's Wonderful • What'll I Do? • White Christmas • and more.
00700637 Solo Guitar...........................$14.99

CHRISTMAS CAROLS

26 songs, including: Auld Lang Syne • Away in a Manger • Deck the Hall • God Rest Ye Merry, Gentlemen • Good King Wenceslas • Here We Come A-Wassailing • It Came upon the Midnight Clear • Joy to the World • O Holy Night • O Little Town of Bethlehem • Silent Night • Toyland • We Three Kings of Orient Are • and more.
00701697 Solo Guitar...........................$14.99

CHRISTMAS JAZZ

21 songs, including Auld Lang Syne • Baby, It's Cold Outside • Cool Yule • Have Yourself a Merry Little Christmas • I've Got My Love to Keep Me Warm • Mary, Did You Know? • Santa Baby • Sleigh Ride • White Christmas • Winter Wonderland • and more.
00171334 Solo Guitar...........................$15.99

DISNEY SONGS

27 songs, including: Beauty and the Beast • Can You Feel the Love Tonight • Candle on the Water • Colors of the Wind • A Dream Is a Wish Your Heart Makes • Heigh-Ho • Some Day My Prince Will Come • Under the Sea • When You Wish upon a Star • A Whole New World (Aladdin's Theme) • Zip-A-Dee-Doo-Dah • and more.
00701902 Solo Guitar...........................$14.99

DUKE ELLINGTON

25 songs, including: C-Jam Blues • Caravan • Do Nothin' Till You Hear from Me • Don't Get Around Much Anymore • I Got It Bad and That Ain't Good • I'm Just a Lucky So and So • In a Sentimental Mood • It Don't Mean a Thing (If It Ain't Got That Swing) • Mood Indigo • Perdido • Prelude to a Kiss • Satin Doll • and more.
00700636 Solo Guitar $14.99

FAVORITE STANDARDS

27 songs, including: All the Way • Autumn in New York • Blue Skies • Cheek to Cheek • Don't Get Around Much Anymore • How Deep Is the Ocean • I'll Be Seeing You • Isn't It Romantic? • It Could Happen to You • The Lady Is a Tramp • Moon River • Speak Low • Take the "A" Train • Willow Weep for Me • Witchcraft • and more.
00699756 Solo Guitar...........................$17.99

JAZZ BALLADS

27 songs, including: Body and Soul • Darn That Dream • Easy to Love (You'd Be So Easy to Love) • Here's That Rainy Day • In a Sentimental Mood • Misty • My Foolish Heart • My Funny Valentine • The Nearness of You • Stella by Starlight • Time After Time • The Way You Look Tonight • When Sunny Gets Blue • and more.
00699755 Solo Guitar...........................$16.99

LATIN STANDARDS

27 Latin favorites, including: Água De Beber (Water to Drink) • Desafinado • The Girl from Ipanema • How Insensitive (Insensatez) • Little Boat • Meditation • One Note Samba (Samba De Uma Nota So) • Poinciana • Quiet Nights of Quiet Stars • Samba De Orfeu • So Nice (Summer Samba) • Wave • and more.
00699754 Solo Guitar...........................$16.99

Order online at **halleonard.com**

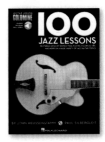

CLASSICAL GUITAR

INSTRUCTIONAL BOOKS & METHODS AVAILABLE FROM HAL LEONARD

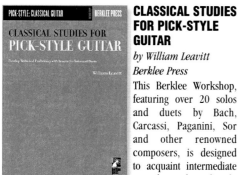

CLASSICAL STUDIES FOR PICK-STYLE GUITAR
by William Leavitt
Berklee Press
This Berklee Workshop, featuring over 20 solos and duets by Bach, Carcassi, Paganini, Sor and other renowned composers, is designed to acquaint intermediate to advanced pick-style guitarists with some of the excellent classical music that is adaptable to pick-style guitar. With study and practice, this workshop will increase a player's knowledge and proficiency on this formidable instrument.
50449440...$14.99

ÉTUDES SIMPLES FOR GUITAR
by Leo Brouwer
Editions Max Eschig
This new, completely revised and updated edition includes critical commentary and performance notes. Each study is accompanied by an introduction that illustrates its principal musical features and technical objectives, complete with suggestions and preparatory exercises.
50565810 Book/CD Pack.......................................$26.99

FIRST BOOK FOR THE GUITAR
by Frederick Noad
G. Schirmer, Inc.
A beginner's manual to the classical guitar. Uses a systematic approach using the interesting solo and duet music written by Noad, one of the world's foremost guitar educators. No musical knowledge is necessary. Student can progress by simple stages. Many of the exercises are designed for a teacher to play with the students. Will increase student's enthusiasm, therefore increasing the desire to take lessons.
50334370 Part 1.......................................$12.99
50334520 Part 2.......................................$18.99
50335160 Part 3.......................................$16.99
50336760 Complete Edition.................................$32.99

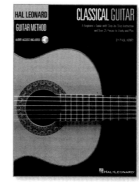

HAL LEONARD CLASSICAL GUITAR METHOD
INCLUDES TAB
by Paul Henry
This comprehensive and easy-to-use beginner's guide uses the music of the master composers to teach you the basics of the classical style and technique. Includes pieces by Beethoven, Bach, Mozart, Schumann, Giuliani, Carcassi, Bathioli, Aguado, Tarrega, Purcell, and more. Includes all the basics plus info on PIMA technique, two- and three-part music, time signatures, key signatures, articulation, free stroke, rest stroke, composers, and much more.
00697376 Book/Online Audio (no tab) $16.99
00142652 Book/Online Audio (with tab) $17.99

A MODERN APPROACH TO CLASSICAL GUITAR
by Charles Duncan
This multi-volume method was developed to allow students to study the art of classical guitar within a new, more contemporary framework. For private, class or self-instruction.

00695114 Book 1 – Book Only...............................$8.99
00695113 Book 1 – Book/Online Audio................$12.99
00699204 Book 1 – Repertoire Book Only............$11.99
00699205 Book 1 – Repertoire Book/Online Audio .$16.99
00695116 Book 2 – Book Only...............................$8.99
00695115 Book 2 – Book/Online Audio................$12.99
00699208 Book 2 – Repertoire.............................$12.99
00699202 Book 3 – Book Only...............................$9.99
00695117 Book 3 – Book/Online Audio................$14.99
00695119 Composite Book/CD Pack....................$32.99

100 GRADED CLASSICAL GUITAR STUDIES
Selected and Graded by Frederick Noad
Frederick Noad has selected 100 studies from the works of three outstanding composers of the classical period: Sor, Giuliani, and Carcassi. All these studies are invaluable for developing both right hand and left hand skills. Students and teachers will find this book invaluable for making technical progress. In addition, they will build a repertoire of some of the most melodious music ever written for the guitar.
14023154...$29.99

CHRISTOPHER PARKENING GUITAR METHOD
THE ART & TECHNIQUE OF THE CLASSICAL GUITAR
Guitarists will learn basic classical technique by playing over 50 beautiful classical pieces, 26 exercises and 14 duets, and through numerous photos and illustrations. The method covers: rudiments of classical technique, note reading and music theory, selection and care of guitars, strategies for effective practicing, and much more!
00696023 Book 1/Online Audio $22.99
00695228 Book 1 (No Audio) $17.99
00696024 Book 2/Online Audio $22.99
00695229 Book 2 (No Audio) $17.99

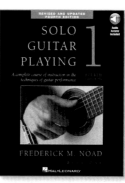

SOLO GUITAR PLAYING
by Frederick M. Noad
Solo Guitar Playing can teach even the person with no previous musical training how to progress from simple single-line melodies to mastery of the guitar as a solo instrument. Fully illustrated with diagrams, photographs, and over 200 musical exercises and repertoire selections, these books offer instruction in every phase of classical guitar playing.
14023147 Book 1/Online Audio $34.99
14023153 Book 1 (Book Only) $24.99
14023151 Book 2 (Book Only) $19.99

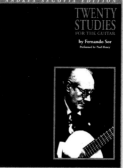

TWENTY STUDIES FOR THE GUITAR
ANDRÉS SEGOVIA EDITION
by Fernando Sor
Performed by Paul Henry
20 studies for the classical guitar written by Beethoven's contemporary, Fernando Sor, revised, edited and fingered by the great classical guitarist Andres Segovia. These essential repertoire pieces continue to be used by teachers and students to build solid classical technique. Features 50-minute demonstration audio.
00695012 Book/Online Audio $22.99
00006363 Book Only..$9.99

HAL•LEONARD®
Order these and more publications from your favorite music retailer at
halleonard.com

Prices, contents and availability subject to change without notice.

0123
005